The Story of a Football

It Starts with Leather

Robin Nelson

Lerner Publications ◆ Minneapolis

Lerner Publications Company
An imprint of Lerner Publishing Group, Inc.
241 First Avenue North
Minneapolis, MN 55401 USA

For reading levels and more information, look up this title at www.lernerbooks.com.

Image credits: RichVintage/Getty Images, p. 3; AP Photo/Amy Sancetta, pp. 5, 23 (top right); AP Photo/Kiichiro Sato, pp. 7, 21, 23 (lower left); Jim West/Alamy Stock Photo, pp. 9, 11, 13; AP Photo/Charles Rex Arbogast, pp. 15, 23 (lower right); courtesy of Madison Sport, pp. 17, 23 (top left); Matt Sullivan/Reuters/Alamy Stock Photo, p. 19; LWA/Dann Tardif/Getty Images, p. 22. Cover images: Mtsaride/Shutterstock.com (football), Peter Versnel/Shutterstock.com (leather).

Main body text set in Mikado a Medium.
Typeface provided by HVD Fonts.

Library of Congress Cataloging-in-Publication Data

Names: Nelson, Robin, 1971- author.
Title: The story of a football: it starts with leather / Robin Nelson.
Description: Minneapolis : Lerner Publications, [2022] | Series: Step by step | Includes bibliographical references and index. | Audience: Ages 4–8 | Audience: Grades K–1 | Summary: "How does a piece of leather become a football? Readers discover the process step by step with clear text and photos demonstrating each part of the process"—Provided by publisher.
Identifiers: LCCN 2021000083 (print) | LCCN 2021000084 (ebook) | ISBN 9781728428239 (library binding) | ISBN 9781728431635 (paperback) | ISBN 9781728430874 (ebook)
Subjects: LCSH: Footballs—Design and construction—Juvenile literature.
Classification: LCC GV749.B34 N48 2022 (print) | LCC GV749.B34 (ebook) | DDC 796.33—dc23

LC record available at https://lccn.loc.gov/2021000083
LC ebook record available at https://lccn.loc.gov/2021000084

Manufactured in the United States of America
1-49360-49464-3/17/2021

Touchdown!

How are footballs made?

First, a worker cuts
the leather.

Next, a machine stamps the panels.

The panels
are weighed.

Then a lining is added.

Next, a worker sews the panels.

A worker turns the ball right side out.

Then a worker
adds the bladder.

Next, a worker laces
the football.

NFL

NEW ENGLAND
PATRIOTS

ATIONAL FOOTBALL LEAGUE

Finally, the football is inflated.

Let's play!

Picture Glossary

bladder

leather

panel

worker

Learn More

Murray, Julie. *Football*. Minneapolis: Abdo Kids, 2018.

Nelson, Robin. *The Story of a Baseball Bat: It Starts with Wood*. Minneapolis: Lerner Publications, 2021.

Rebman, Nick. *Football*. Mendota Heights, MN: Focus Readers, 2018.

Index